50 Uses for Your Cat

Cat Skills Uncovered!

Written by

Jay Groce
Francesca Peppiatt
Paul Seaburn

new seasons®

1 To show you a way to relax when you're on pins and needles

2 🐾 To hold the boards together until the glue sets

3 🐾 To smooth out dog-eared pages

4 🐾 To assure Virginia that there *is* a Santa Claus

5 🐾 To remind you that some boots are *not* made for walking

6 🐾 To start a yawn chain reaction

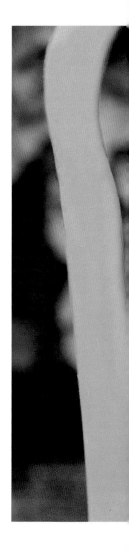

7 🐾 To keep you from getting between a rock and a hard place

8 🐾 To help clean fur coats

9 🐾 To turn a catnap on its head

10

To find amusement in the smallest of things

11 🐾 To teach a young dog new tricks

12 🐾 To give a gentle reminder that your library could use a few cat books

13 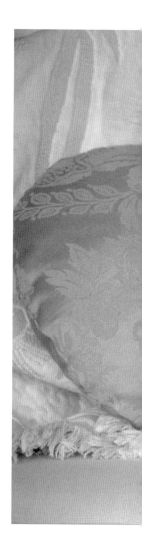 To put the *spread* in *bedspread*

14 🐾 To prove that the lawn really does need to be mowed

15 🐾 To help you turn over a new leaf

16 🐾 To wait for a signal from the home planet

17 🐾 To watch your every move

19 🐾 To help when
mom makes
you drink skim

20 🐾 To get fat enough to obstruct the view of nosy neighbors

21 🐾 To block you from sitting on an exposed spring

22 🐾 To give the eyes in the back of your head a rest

23 🐾 To play dead to fool the guests

24 To recommend an easy course in basket-making

25 🐾 To be your paperweight

26 🐾 To dispel the myth that cats are naturally clean

27 To put the *fur* in *furniture*

28 🐾 To shred the
bills but leave
the checks

29 🐾 To warn the mail carrier before the dog does something dumb

30

To keep you warm on
a cool spring day

31 🐾 To play a new game of cat and mouse

33

To make sure
there's enough sugar

34 To remind you to separate the whites from the colors

35 🐾 To guard your bear necessities

36 🐾 To keep firefighters busy

37

To help you
get back in
the saddle

38 🐾 To protect you
from bad luck

39 🐾 To remind you that everything's covered

40 🐾 To suggest that you not keep things bottled up

41 🐾 To be your muse

42 🐾 To have a
crazier hair
day than you

43 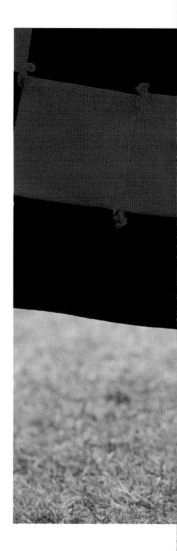 To stop you from pulling a loose thread

44 🐾 To sprinkle good cheer

45 🐾 To magnify your good qualities

46 🐾 To test if turkey
makes cats
sleepy, too

47 🐾 To protect you from accidents while wearing high heels

48

To get in your face
when you need it

🐾 To make sure nothing
is hiding *anywhere*

50  To miss you when you're gone